Contents

Our Bodies

Our beating heart

The heart is one of the most important organs in the human body. It continuously pumps blood around our body through blood vessels. We now know that blood is made up of four main ingredients:

- red blood cells – these carry oxygen to our muscles and other organs
- plasma – this carries waste products like carbon dioxide
- white blood cells – these help fight infections by destroying the germs they find
- platelets – these help the blood form scabs when we cut ourselves.

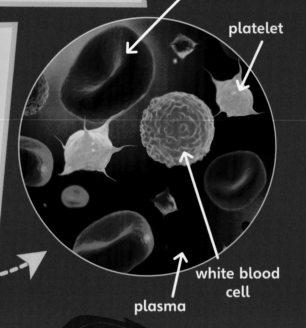

red blood cell

platelet

white blood cell

plasma

Did you know?

Your pulse is a pressure wave from your heartbeat. Can you find your pulse? How many places on your body can you find your pulse?

Things to do

Fill a washing-up liquid bottle with water. Squeeze it hard and measure how far the water goes in the air. Your heart could pump water about 230 metres high!

A history of the heart

We didn't always know about blood and how it was transported around our bodies! The ancient Egyptians believed that the heart was the home of the soul.

The 'weighing of the heart' ceremony happened when a person died.

In ancient Rome, Greek surgeon Galen knew that blood was carried in veins and arteries. It wasn't until 1628 that an English doctor called William Harvey discovered that blood circulated through the body and that it was the heart that pumped the blood around.

William Harvey

Today, surgeons know so much about how the heart works that they are able to transplant hearts from donors to people who need a new heart to survive.

South African doctor, Christiaan Barnard, performed the first human heart transplant in 1967.

Circulating blood

Look at this diagram of the heart.

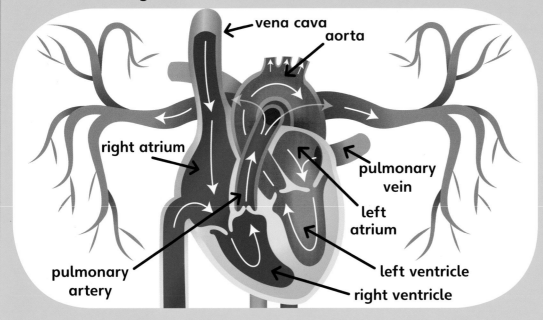

vena cava

aorta

right atrium

pulmonary vein

left atrium

pulmonary artery

left ventricle

right ventricle

The heart has four chambers. There are four blood vessels or tubes coming in or out of the chambers. Which ones do you think carry blood into the heart? What do the other tubes do?

Three types of blood vessels carry blood around your body.

Arteries
These have thick elastic walls and carry blood away from the heart.

Veins
These have thinner walls and carry blood back to the heart.

Capillaries
These are very thin and carry blood to and from arteries and veins.

Did you know?

Your heart beats about 3 000 million times during your lifetime.

AND ...

If you stretched out all of your blood vessels they would reach a quarter of the way to the Moon!

Speed up, slow down

When we exercise, our heart beats faster. Try it yourself. Find your pulse and measure it when you are resting. Now exercise hard for a few minutes and take another measurement. Are the numbers of beats per minute the same?

When we exercise, our heart needs to pump blood around our body faster. Why do you think this is?

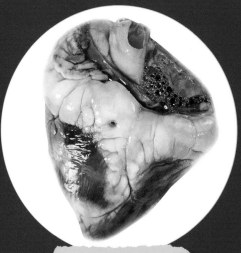

a human heart

Find out

The human heart beats about 70 times a minute when we are resting. A hummingbird's heart beats 1 300 times each minute. A blue whale's beats only 10 times each minute! Is there a pattern between the number of heart beats per minute and the size of an animal?

Eating for health

Why aren't you allowed chocolate and chips for dinner every day? Food keeps our body healthy, but it needs to be the right sort of food, not just whatever we fancy.

Some foods are essential to keep us healthy. Some foods give us energy and others help us to grow and repair our bodies. Eating different things makes food interesting and helps make sure we have a balanced diet.

Can you remember the food groups that humans need to eat?

Things to do

Make a list of the fruit and vegetables you usually eat. Over the next week, every time you eat one tick it on the list. Make a chart to show which fruit and vegetables you eat the most.

Find out

Energy in food is measured in calories. A 10-year-old child needs about 2 400 calories a day. That's more than an adult needs! Why do you think that is?

Drugs and you

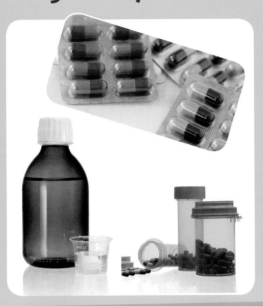

To stay healthy we not only need to eat the right sort of foods in the right quantities, but we also need to avoid substances that could cause us harm.

A drug is a substance that causes our bodies to change. Drugs can change the way we feel, make our heart beat faster or make our thinking slower. Some drugs are addictive; once we start using them it may be very hard to stop.

Medicines are also drugs but they are only used to prevent or treat illness.

Did you know?

Tobacco smoke contains carbon monoxide which is a poisonous gas.

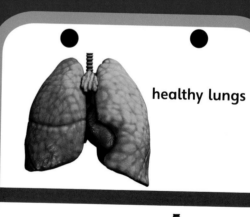

healthy lungs

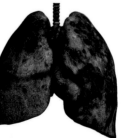

lungs affected by smoking

Light and Sight

What is light?

You cannot hear it, taste it, feel it or smell it ... but you can see it. What is it? Light!

The Sun is the main source of light on Earth. A light source is something that makes its own light, like a torch or a candle flame or the Sun. Some things that look bright, like cat's eyes, high visibility jackets and the Moon, only reflect light.

How fast does light go?

Light travels very quickly! It can travel up to 300 000 kilometres in a second. That means in only one second, light could travel around the world seven times! It is the fastest thing we know.

Light's journey

Light travels in straight lines from its source. When it meets an object, it changes direction. When light hits something very flat, smooth or shiny like a mirror it bounces off. This is called reflecting.

Things to do

Draw a circle on a piece of paper. Now draw around the edge of the circle seven times. Do it as fast as you can. Get a friend to time how long you take. Imagine now that your circle was the size of the circumference of the world and that you had to go round that seven times in one second. That's how fast light can go!

How do we see?

Have you ever heard people talking about someone having 'piercing eyes' or 'throwing a glance'? Everyday language can make it seem as if our eyes are actively producing mysterious beams which let us see, but this is not true. Our eyes receive light that has been reflected off the objects around us, then our brain makes sense of what we see.

Did you know?

About 1000 years ago, Persian scientist, Al Hazan, knew we saw objects because of reflected light travelling to our eyes.

Things to do

Take a mirror into a totally dark place. Why can't you see anything in it?

Bouncing beams

Most smooth surfaces, like paper or the top of a desk, are actually quite uneven. Light is reflected off them in all directions.

Very smooth surfaces like mirrors reflect light in a more regular way.

Did you know?

Neil Armstrong and Buzz Aldrin, the first astronauts to land on the Moon, left a mirror the size of a tea tray on the Moon's surface. Scientists were able to use this to reflect a laser beam back to Earth 380 000 km away.

How can your clothes keep you safe?

People who work around traffic wear special clothes so that drivers can see them more easily. This is often bright yellow with reflective strips.

What is the best colour to wear to be seen at night?

Look at these children. Whose clothes are better for cycling at night? Why? Which is the best bike for cycling at night? Why?

Things to do

Hold some pieces of different coloured card upright on a white surface. Shine a strong torch onto the card to produce a reflection of the light on the white surface. Which colour reflects the most light? Which reflects the least?

Predict it!

Other children say:

If you move the lamp the shadow will move.

If you move the lamp nearer to the screen the shadow will get smaller.

The shadow will get bigger if you move the puppet closer to the screen.

The shadow is the biggest when the puppet is closest to the lamp.

I don't think it matters where the lamp is.

Which do you think is the best prediction? Why?

The classification system

Carl Linnaeus

Carl Linnaeus was born in 1707 in Sweden. He was a highly respected scientist who suggested that all living things could be classified into large groups called kingdoms. He called two of the main kingdoms animals and plants.

Today we know that some of the creatures in Linnaeus' original work do not actually exist. He suggested that there was a group of creatures known as Paradoxa. This group included dragons, unicorns and the phoenix!

Carl Linnaeus

These mythical creatures are featured in Linnaeus' work but are not included in today's classification systems.

Find out
What else can you find out about Carl Linnaeus' life?

The animal kingdom

Linnaeus identified two subgroups within the animal kingdom: vertebrates and invertebrates.

Vertebrates include mammals, reptiles, birds, amphibians and fish.

Invertebrates include insects, arachnids, worms and molluscs.

The plant kingdom

Linnaeus identified two subgroups within the plant kingdom: flowering plants and non-flowering plants.

Flowering plants include all types of flowering plant from daisies right through to horse chestnut trees.

Non-flowering plants include some trees that produce cones and mosses that produce spores instead of flowers.

Evaluate it!

Two children wanted to find out whether mould would grow more quickly on different types of bread.

I've got some sliced brown bread, sliced white bread and a wholemeal bread roll. We can use these.

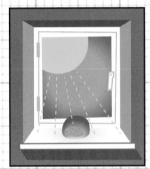

I think the mould will grow better in a warm, light place, so I'm going to put the bread roll on the window sill.

I think the mould will grow better if it is kept moist, so I'll spray the white bread with water and leave it in a cupboard.

Let's put the brown bread in the fridge to see if it stops the mould from growing.

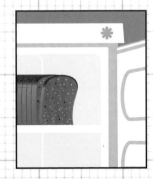

What could the children do to get better evidence about the way mould grows on different types of bread?

What safety precautions should the children have taken during this investigation?

	White sliced bread in cupboard and sprayed with water	Brown sliced bread in fridge	Wholemeal bread roll on window sill
1 day	nothing	nothing	nothing
2 weeks	some mould	nothing	small amount of mould
3 weeks	lots of mould	small amount of mould	some mould

Things to do

What other investigations could you do to find out what makes mould grow better? Make sure you plan and carry out your investigation safely.

Make a composter!

You will need:

- three large plastic bottles
- scissors
- sticky tape
- netting/old pair of tights
- elastic band
- 'browns' (newspaper or wood shavings)
- 'greens' (vegetable or fruit scraps).

- sticky tack
- needle
- compost

1 Cut the first bottle in half.

2 Cut 5 cm off the bottom of the second and third bottles and remove the lids.

3 Cover the opening of the second bottle with netting and secure it in place using the elastic band.

4 Turn the second bottle upside down and place it inside the bottom half of the first bottle with the neck pointing downwards.

5 Place the compost material inside the second bottle. Add a small amount of water to lightly moisten your mixture.

6 Using a large lump of sticky tack and a large needle, pierce several holes into the sides of the third bottle.

7 Keep the third bottle the right way up and place it on top of the second bottle. Fasten both bottles together using sticky tape.

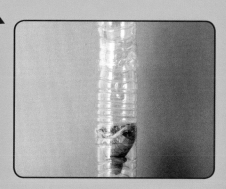

8 Place your composter in a warm, safe place.

Things to do

Make your compost from a mixture of 'greens' and 'browns'. Your compost will turn into a slimy mess if you use just 'greens' in your composter!

Electricity explained

We can see, feel and hear the results of electricity, but we can't actually see what happens inside the wires. Scientists often use models and stories to explain what happens. In each model the different parts of the circuit are represented by different things.

Look at these four different models. Which one do you think is the best?

1

Water flowing in a pipe

In this model, the battery is represented by a pump pumping water (electricity) around a pipe (wire).

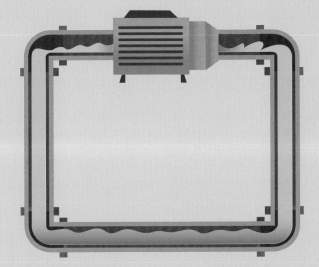

Part of circuit	How it's represented
battery	pump
wire	water pipe
electricity flowing/electric current	water

2

Passing balls around a circle of people

Stand in a circle with some of your friends. Each of you should hold a small ball.

To show the flow of current, each person passes their ball to the person next to them in a clockwise direction. Everyone should pass the ball with their left hand and take the new ball from the person to their right with their right hand. Everyone should then pass the ball across their body and pass it on again.

The battery is modelled by one person saying 'pass' repeatedly.

Part of circuit	How it's represented
battery	person saying pass
wire	people
electricity flowing/electric current	small balls

3

The rope loop

The circuit is modelled using a long piece of string held by enough people to make a loop. The hands holding the string are open allowing the string to move easily through them.

One person models the battery and pulls the string. Another person closes their hands a little. This person is the thin wire in a light bulb. They stop the string moving easily because they offer some resistance. Ask them what they feel. They should feel their hands warm up. This is like the wire in the bulb which glows as it gets hot.

My hands are getting warm!

Things to do

With a group of friends try this model for electricity. Be careful not to let your hands get too hot stop when you are gripping the string.

Part of circuit	How it's represented
battery	person pulling the string
wire	open hands
thin wire in bulb (filament)	closed hands
electricity flowing/electric current	string moving around the circuit

Find out

Research other models to explain how electricity works and share them with your friends.

4

Little cups of raisins

This model is like the ball pass. Instead of passing balls, you put three or four raisins in small cups. People stand in a circle passing the cups of raisins around the circle when signalled to do so.

One person acts as the bulb and eats a raisin from each cup when it reaches them. The bulb is lit whilst the cups have raisins to offer. Once they have run out, the bulb will no longer light up.

Part of circuit	How it's represented
battery	person saying pass
electricity flowing or electric current	raisins
bulb	person eating raisins

Record it!

Engineers, electricians and scientists all use the same symbols for different parts of electrical circuits. They do this to avoid making mistakes.

Here are the symbols used in circuit diagrams:

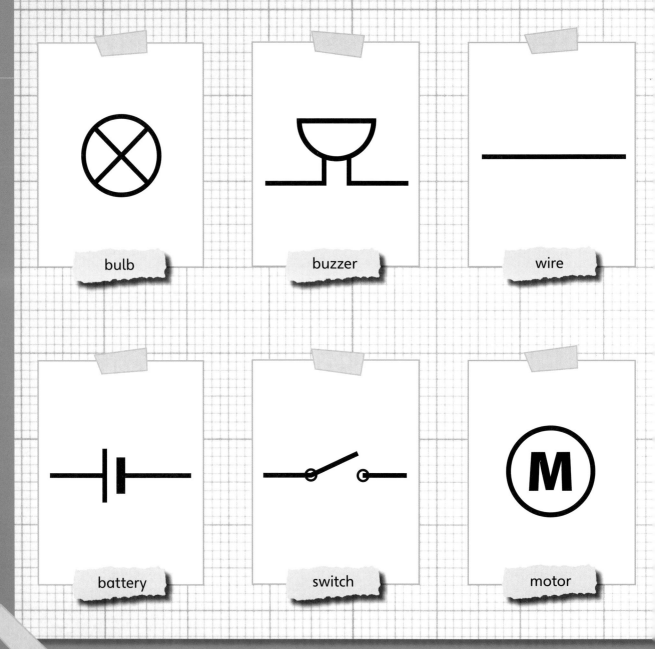

bulb

buzzer

wire

battery

switch

motor

Look at these circuit diagrams. Can you describe what would happen in each of them?

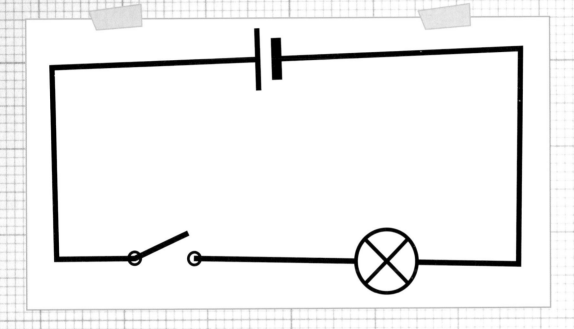

Evolution and Inheritance

Fossil mysteries

People have always wondered about how life began on Earth.

About 200 years ago, scientists began to ask questions about fossils. They wondered why fossils of giant sea creatures were found on the tops of mountains and why these giant creatures were not found alive anymore. Perhaps Earth had not always been the same. Perhaps Earth and the creatures living on it had changed over time. Perhaps these changes had been going on for a very long time.

A blast from the past!

We know now that Earth is very, very old; about 4.54 billion years old.

TODAY

First human: 3 000 000

First dinosaurs and first mammals: 200 000 000

First plant on land: 450 000 000

First single celled organism: 3 500 000,000

Earth is formed: 4 600 000 000

Did you know?

The earliest animal fossils are a mere 650 million years old. That's very young in geological time!

Find out

Find out how fossils are formed.

She Sells Sea Shells By The Sea Shore

She sells sea shells by the sea shore.
The shells she sells are sea shells I'm sure.
For if she sells sea shells by the sea shore,
Then I'm sure she sells sea shore shells.

This tongue twister is about Mary Anning (1799-1847). She was one of the first palaeontologists (a scientist who studies fossils).

Mary was only twelve when she discovered the first ichthyosaur fossil in the cliffs at Lyme Regis on the south coast of England. She wasn't trained in science and came from a poor family, but she became one of the greatest palaeontologists ever known.

Alike, but different

Do you look a bit like your brother or sister? Does your mum look a bit like your grandmother? Families tend to share similar characteristics like skin colour, type of hair and face shape. They pass these features on to their children. We say that features are 'inherited'.

Gradual change

This happens in nature too. Every species (group of plants or animals which are similar and are able to produce young together) passes on characteristics to the next generation.

Not every baby is identical to its parent; they all vary slightly. Some variations give individuals an advantage.

We're all a bit different. I have the best eyesight and reaction time so I'll catch the most mice.

Successful variations give those animals a better chance to survive and pass on these helpful characteristics to future generations. Over many generations very noticeable changes or 'adaptations' can be seen. Eventually the accumulation of these small changes can result in an entirely new species. We call this process evolution.

Find out

Find out about selective breeding in dogs. Why are there so many different types of dog?

Evolution revolution!

Charles Darwin (1809-1882) was one of the world's greatest scientists. He had an amazing and exciting life studying nature and travelling all over the world. His ideas completely changed the way people thought about living things.

The voyage of the Beagle

Aged 22, Darwin sailed around the world on the ship HMS Beagle. When the ship docked, he would get off and explore!

On the Galapagos Islands in the Pacific Ocean, Darwin found some unusual animals like huge tortoises and lizards that could swim in the sea!

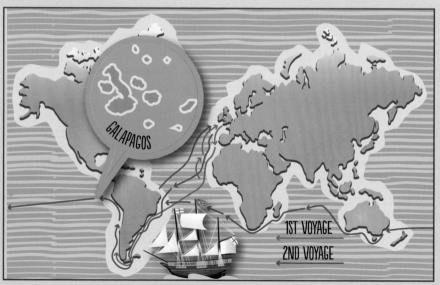

GALAPAGOS

1ST VOYAGE

2ND VOYAGE

Darwin's big idea

Darwin thought that individual animals and plants competed with each other for food, water and space – the things they need to live. They were in competition with each other for these resources and struggled to survive. He thought those with features best fitted to survive in particular environments were naturally selected.

Did you know?

Darwin was not a good sailor and was horribly sea sick on the voyage of the Beagle.

Darwin's ideas caused a sensation! People used to think that species were completely separate from each other. Darwin explained how all living things, including humans, came originally from the same living things. He said that those living things had changed over time to form the millions of different species we see today.

Find out

Many people think that a man called Alfred Russell Wallace is as important as Charles Darwin. Find out about Wallace and his ideas.

Index